DETERIORATE

FIRST EDITION

ISBN 978-1-7371427-0-6

DETERIORATE

BY

MICHELLE MARIE JACQUOT

CONTENTS

The State of Mistakes

Every Floor Is A Smoking Floor

Sunset & Crescent Heights

Sparknotes

Blank

Rules of Engagement

And I Still Have Money For Starbucks

Spears

Tear

Personal Best

Your Advantage

ALSO BY MICHELLE MARIE JACQUOT

Death of a Good Girl

THIS BOOK WAS CREATED ON A COMPUTER

I hope you enjoy this e-book
about hating anything "e"
I hope you turn your phone off
after reading
and never pick it up again

Love,

The Irony
and Me

Future Libraries

I would pay one million anything
to find one human staying sane
My soul is going broke
from meeting bodies missing brains
Robots seeking validation
for tickets they refuse to pay
Who can't press a heart shaped button
if it's not of someone's face

If you're not on top of someone famous
No one cares about your day
Shut up and show us what you ate for breakfast
Have no opinion on the way
Tell us what you look like
Not a word of what you think
Only tell me what your age is
Your sex
Your height
Your weight

The new training is as follows
I haven't read it, but neither have they

Step one, forget how to live
Step two, unlearn how to read

I wonder what they teach in schools these days
and what kinds of robots
these robots
will breed

This poem has no title

and no words

in between

but

no matter

no one listens through to the end

they either skip directly to it

or skip the whole thing altogether

at least someone is skipping something
so it can still feel like the 90's

I lied

the title of this poem is now

Jumping Rope

The New Attention Song

Maybe I'll start a garage band
called The New Attention Span

Though I can't remember the last time
I was actually in a garage

My childhood home, playing
ping pong, ping pong

Maybe I'll make an album
filled with only five second songs
but even that would be an album
and five seconds too long

Sing Along

Did you know you can change the words
to any law or fact or song?
If you get enough numb people mumbling
they will repeat anything you want

(and really believe that was the way
it always was)

I guess we change the words now
to hundred-year-old songs
without letting anyone in the copyright office know
and even the writers sing along

Has anyone else noticed what's been going on?

Ten O'Clock News

Your cell phone is dying
hurry up and go charge it
before you do

Just to be sure you have enough
battery left for the broadcast

Wouldn't it be awful if it came
your time to die and nobody
~~really~~ knew ~~you~~?

Correction

The problem with technology
and making notes on the interstate
is the constant rearranging
of what it thinks I have to say

the word *porn*
for the word *poem*
An example from today

Who do you think I am?
If I wanted to write about porn
you would know about it, trust me

and you can't correct what never will be anyway

Do not change the words
from my mouth
to my screen
just because you're unsure
about what *you* want to scream

The Blue Light

I have lost my appetite
and will, over time
my eyesight
from advertisements selling glasses
to shield me from the blue light
emanating from a box
making me go slowly blind
in more ways than one
come to find, it's by design

Why are you selling me
something
on something
I need protecting
from in the first place?

Would you poison yourself
on purpose
under any other circumstance?

The State of Mistakes

Remove yourself
Expose yourself
Get out of your own way
Become too thin
Put on some weight
Love yourself
But only for a day
We'll hate you if you say too much
Or take up much more space
It's too expensive to be proud
Square feet is precious in a place
where you're only allowed
to be loud
about certain things
but say the right thing with your head
tilted a little to the left
and we'll paint giant x's in red
across your face
while keeping very safe the proof
of any little thing
we might be able to use
as a knife one day

Gathering the evidence
Hunting for mistakes
As if the world will never change
As if people never change
or grow old or kind or want to make
apologies or peace
I would like to think
There will come a time
When finishing this sentence
Would
Actually
even be worth it
and I wouldn't be crucified
for what you think the end of it might be
before I've even thought it

Sorry in advance, for… I'm not sure what

Yet

Even I don't know
where that sentence train was going
Don't shoot the messenger
or steal his wallet
There's nothing inside to take

He's just as stupid as you

Every Floor Is A Smoking Floor

All the rooms that come
with a spare bed
for human error
have been sold out
tonight, here
and in all
foreseeable
futures

Sunset & Crescent Heights

It's hard to write about life
when you're only ever surrounded by
people trying to imitate it

Sparknotes

Living in a story
of a film
based on a book
we said we saw
or bought, but didn't

Yet still assume we know the end

Or better, pretend it doesn't have one

That it's not really coming as soon as they said

Drinking twice a day
from the fountain of the youth
Do we think the kids will be alright
if we leave them nothing to lose?

So the movie turns to horror
but looks more like a comedy sketch
From the outside it's absurdly both,
The World headlines read like this—

*"Los Angeles is burning
and it made the front-page news!
But sad to say, no one made it out alive
They were all too busy forgetting dying,
too busy taking photos
of the view"*

"Los Angeles is burning
and it made the front-page news!
But sad to say, no one made it out alive
They were all too busy forgetting dying,
too busy taking photos
of the view"

d to say, no one made it o
vere all too busy forgettir
sy taking photos

Purposely

left

blank

What

do

you

think?

Whatever followed

was courtesy

of your own

right

brain

Rules of Engagement

This world is just a simulation that has real
life consequences. That will bleed you clean
and dry of your heart and of your paychecks

Judged by arbitrary rules, art becomes a
numbers game. Who gets to make it is
determined by a figure by a name

Here on earth, statistics tell us which work
will see the light of day. Gifts are given out
at random. Not by merit, but for stage

You can join the club if you agree to the
expenses. Just sell your soul, betray your gut,
show some leg and smash your lenses—

And if you attempt to come to any one of
your own senses, it will only ever meet you
with 99 cent devastation

And I Still Have Money For Starbucks

It's cheaper than a can of coke
to get your dreams crushed these days
I would know, I've drank and crushed
one of both every conceivable way

Spears

I'd like to rip my hair out

one by one and count them all

to have something more living

to look at in my palm

to hold something other than

someone else's life

something moving

something when you touch feels a little too hot

let's do it together

one by one

on the count of three

two by two

two by two

four by four

if you've got the balls

let's be like Britney

make people think we've lost it

and go bald

be like Britney

make people think you've gone insane

when you've only just stopped

Tear

this page out

if you please

please

change

something

anything

at

all

Personal Best

Please let me keep my insides
inside where they belong
My body may not be a temple
but of it I've grown quietly fond

These limbs that let me wander
Hold my head up when the rest is down
I've been feeding, reading stories to it
for almost twenty-six years now

Please don't make me burn my house
and all its stories to the ground
It's the only one I have, the one thing I'd take with me
if I had to leave right now

If I'm forced to give it all away
there will be nothing to be found
They'll dig up a still life portrait of a girl
and scratch their heads
because
she was pretty
but she's missing a mouth

Let me hold my dignity
as I watch the world go down
Even it's foolish, even if
words won't save me now

Even if I end up buried
with just some paper and that mouth

Let me dig my way to China
Even if we're headed toward the ground

Even if we end up sinking
All my screaming for nothing
I want to say at the very least
I tried my hardest not to drown

Even if I'm known
as the girl who thought she could escape
this inevitable sinking, grow gills
somehow

And I never let anyone or anything turn my insides out

Your Advantage

Now is the perfect time
to learn how to dance
as if they're not watching
because, simply, they aren't
and if they are, anything too embarrassing
will be forgotten
almost as soon as they saw it
I promise

they're only worried about themselves
and what they might look like
and these are the times
when that part works out pretty nice

ABOUT THE AUTHOR

Michelle Marie Jacquot is a writer from Los Angeles, California. Her debut poetry collection *Death of a Good Girl* was published in the fall of 2019. She does not have a love–hate relationship with social media, simply hate.

You can follow her ironically to piss off the publisher who told her to "try again when [she has] 50,000 followers."

@michellemariejacquot
@michellejacquot
www.michellemariejacquot.com